# DIABETIC
## RECIPES
### FOR THE HOLIDAYS

Publications International, Ltd.

**Front cover and contents page photography:** Sacco Productions Limited, Chicago
**All other photography:** Audrey Nilsen Photography, Chicago

**Pictured on the front cover:** Roast Turkey with Cranberry Stuffing *(page 42)* and Spicy Southwestern Vegetable Sauté *(page 66).*

**Pictured on the back cover** *(from top to bottom):* Mustard-Crusted Roast Pork *(page 52),* Smoked Salmon Appetizers *(page 14),* Spicy Pumpkin Soup with Green Chili Swirl *(page 26)* and Turtle Cheesecake *(page 88).*

ISBN: 0-7853-3310-X

Manufactured in U.S.A.

8 7 6 5 4 3 2 1

**Microwave Cooking:** Microwave ovens vary in wattage. Use the cooking times as guidelines and check for doneness before adding more time.

# CONTENTS

# Facts About Diabetes

Low-calorie, low-fat, low-cholesterol and low-sodium—buzzwords of the decade and for a good reason. People today are more aware than ever before of the roles that diet and exercise play in maintaining a healthful lifestyle. For people with diabetes and their families, the positive impact good nutrition and physical activity have on well-being is very familiar.

Diabetes is a disease that affects the body's ability to use glucose as a source of fuel. When glucose is utilized improperly, it can build up in the bloodstream, creating higher than normal blood sugar levels. Left unchecked, elevated blood sugar levels may lead to the development of more serious long-term complications like blindness and heart and kidney disease.

Not all cases of diabetes are alike. In fact, the disease presents itself in two very distinct forms—Type I and Type II. Development of diabetes during childhood or adolescence is typical of Type I, or juvenile-onset, diabetes. These individuals are unable to make insulin, a hormone produced by the pancreas that moves glucose from the bloodstream into the body's cells, where it is used as a source of fuel. Daily injections of insulin, coupled with a balanced meal plan, are the focus of treatment.

People who develop Type II diabetes, the more common form of the disease, are typically over the age of 40 and obese. These individuals produce insulin but the amount is insufficient to meet their needs, or their excess weight renders the hormone incapable of adequately performing its functions. Treatment includes balanced eating, moderate weight loss, exercise and, in extreme cases, oral hypoglycemic agents or insulin injections.

### Maximize Health, Minimize Complications

Diabetes increases one's risk of developing high blood pressure and high blood cholesterol levels. Over time, elevated levels may progress to more serious complications, including heart and kidney disease, stroke and hypertension. In fact, research shows that individuals with diabetes are nineteen times more likely to develop kidney disease and four times more likely to suffer from heart disease or a stroke than people who do not have diabetes. While heredity plays a major role in the development of these complications, regular check-ups with your physician and registered dietitian to fine-tune treatment strategies are good ways to help minimize complications. Strategies for treatment vary among individuals, yet overall goals remain the same: achieving and maintaining near-normal blood sugar levels by balancing food intake, insulin and activity; achieving optimal blood cholesterol levels; and improving overall health through good nutrition.

### Balance Is the Key

Achieving optimal nutrition often requires lifestyle changes to balance the intake of nutrients. The United States Department of Agriculture and the United States Department of Health and Human Services developed the Dietary Guidelines to simplify the basics of balanced eating and to help all individuals develop healthful eating plans. Several of the guidelines follow but were adjusted to include the revised 1994 American Diabetes Association's Nutrition Recommendations. Because recommendations are broad, work with your physician and registered dietitian to personalize the guidelines to meet your specific needs.

**Eat a variety of foods.** Energy, protein, vitamins, minerals and fiber are essential for optimal health, but no one food contains them all. Including a wide range of foods in your diet and using fats and oils sparingly throughout the day are easy ways to consume all the nutrients your body needs. Carbohydrate should comprise between 45 and 55 percent of total calories, and protein should contribute between 10 and 20 percent.

**Maintain a healthy weight.** Excess weight can worsen your diabetes and encourages the development of more severe complications. Research shows that shedding 10 to 20 pounds is enough to initiate positive results for obese individuals. Combining a healthful eating plan with physical activity outlined by your health care team is the best medicine for maintaining a healthy weight.

**Choose a diet low in fat, saturated fat and cholesterol.** Fat has more than double the calories of an equal amount of protein or carbohydrate. Thus, diets low in fat make it easier to maintain a desirable weight and decrease the likelihood of developing high blood cholesterol levels. Limit fat to no more than 30 percent of total calories, saturated fat to no more than 10 percent of total calories and daily cholesterol to no more than 300 mg. The 30 percent of calories from fat goal applies to a total diet over time, not to a single food, serving of a recipe or meal.

**Choose a diet with plenty of vegetables, fruits and grain products.**
Vitamins, minerals, fiber and complex carbohydrates abound in these low-fat food choices. Filling up on fiber leaves less room for fat and may produce a slight decrease in blood cholesterol levels. Antioxidants such as beta carotene and the vitamins C and E may protect against heart disease, while magnesium, phosphorous and calcium are minerals that may keep blood pressure levels under control.

**Use sugars in moderation.** The ban on sugar has been lifted for people with diabetes but it is not altogether gone. The new guidelines for simple sugar intake are based on scientific research that indicates that carbohydrate in the form of simple sugars does not raise blood sugar levels more rapidly than any other type of carbohydrate food. What is more important is the total amount of carbohydrate consumed, not the source. However, keep in mind that since simple sugars are loaded with calories, contain no vitamins and minerals, and are linked to the development of cavities, it is still a good idea to limit your intake of simple sugars to no more than 25 percent of total carbohydrate.

**Use salt and sodium in moderation.** Some people with diabetes may be more sensitive to sodium than others, making them more susceptible to high blood pressure. Minimize this risk by limiting sodium intake to no more than 2,400 mg a day (about 1 teaspoon of salt) and choosing single food items with less than 400 mg of sodium and entrées with less than 800 mg of sodium per serving.

### Facts About the Food

The recipes in this publication were designed with people with diabetes in mind. But all are based on the principles of sound nutrition as outlined by the Dietary Guidelines, making them perfect for the entire family. Though the recipes in this publication are not intended as a medically therapeutic program, nor as a substitute for medically approved meal plans for individuals with diabetes, they are low in calories, fat, sodium and cholesterol and will fit easily into an individualized meal plan designed by your physician, registered dietitian and you.

## Facts About the Exchanges

The nutrition information that appears with each recipe was calculated by an independent nutrition consulting firm, and the Dietary Exchanges are based on the Exchange Lists for Meal Planning developed by American Diabetes Association/The American Dietetic Association. Every effort has been made to check the accuracy of these numbers. However, because numerous variables account for a wide range of values in certain foods, all analyses that appear in this book should be considered approximate.

■ The analysis of each recipe includes all the ingredients that are listed in that recipe, *except* ingredients labeled as "optional" or "for garnish." Nutritional analysis is provided for the primary recipe only, not for the recipe variations.

■ If a range is offered for an ingredient, the *first* amount given was used to calculate the nutrition information.

■ If an ingredient is presented with an option ("2 cups hot cooked rice or noodles," for example), the *first* item listed was used to calculate the nutrition information.

■ Foods shown in photographs on the same serving plate and offered as "serve with" suggestions at the end of a recipe are *not* included in the recipe analysis unless they are listed in the ingredient list.

■ Meat should be trimmed of all visible fat because this is reflected in the nutritional analysis.

■ In recipes calling for cooked rice or noodles, the analysis was based on rice or noodles that were prepared without added salt and fat.

■ Most processed foods contain a significant amount of sodium and the amount of sodium is reflected in the analysis. Rinsing canned or jarred processed foods such as beans and tuna under cold running water for one minute eliminates between 40 and 60 percent of added sodium.

# APPETIZERS & DRINKS

## SPICY VEGETABLE QUESADILLAS

*These Southwestern treats are the perfect starters for any party or family gathering. Full of flavor and spice, no one will suspect they're so low in fat.*

Nonstick cooking spray
1 small zucchini, chopped
½ cup chopped green bell pepper
½ cup chopped onion
2 cloves garlic, minced

½ teaspoon ground cumin
½ teaspoon chili powder
8 (6-inch) flour tortillas
1 cup (4 ounces) shredded reduced-fat Cheddar cheese
¼ cup chopped fresh cilantro

**1** Spray large nonstick skillet with cooking spray. Heat over medium heat until hot. Add zucchini, pepper, onion, garlic, cumin and chili powder; cook and stir 3 to 4 minutes or until vegetables are crisp-tender. Remove vegetable mixture and set aside; wipe skillet clean.

**2** Spoon vegetable mixture evenly over half of each tortilla. Sprinkle each evenly with cheese and cilantro. Fold each tortilla in half.

**3** Spray same skillet with cooking spray. Add tortillas and heat 1 to 2 minutes per side over medium heat or until lightly browned. Cut into thirds before serving.

*Makes 8 servings*

### Nutrients per Serving:

| | | | | | |
|---|---|---|---|---|---|
| Calories | 153 (22% calories from fat) | | | | |
| Total Fat | 4 g | Carbohydrate | 23 g | Iron | trace |
| Saturated Fat | 1 g | Dietary Fiber | 1 g | Vitamin A | 56 RE |
| Cholesterol | 8 mg | Protein | 7 g | Vitamin C | 15 mg |
| Sodium | 201 mg | Calcium | 112 mg | Sugar | 1 g |

DIETARY EXCHANGES: 1½ Starch/Bread, ½ Lean Meat, ½ Fat

# PINEAPPLE GINGER SHRIMP COCKTAIL

*Combining the tropical treasures of pineapple and ginger with America's favorite shellfish results in a delectable taste sensation. Cooked, shelled shrimp should look succulent and plump with no hint of ammonia odor. Fresh pineapple spears are available in the produce section of most supermarkets.*

9 fresh pineapple spears (about 1 package), divided
¼ cup all-fruit apricot preserves
1 tablespoon finely chopped onion
½ teaspoon grated fresh ginger

⅛ teaspoon ground black pepper
8 ounces cooked medium shrimp (about 30)
1 red or green bell pepper, cut into 12 strips

**1** Chop 3 pineapple spears into bite-sized pieces; combine with preserves, onion, ginger and black pepper in medium bowl.

**2** Evenly arrange shrimp, bell pepper strips and remaining pineapple spears on 6 small plates lined with lettuce leaves, if desired. Add one spoonful of pineapple mixture to each plate. *Makes 6 servings*

**Nutrients per Serving:**

| Calories | 108 (6% calories from fat) | | | | |
|---|---|---|---|---|---|
| Total Fat | 1 g | Carbohydrate | 20 g | Iron | 2 mg |
| Saturated Fat | trace | Dietary Fiber | 2 g | Vitamin A | 264 RE |
| Cholesterol | 58 mg | Protein | 7 g | Vitamin C | 95 mg |
| Sodium | 69 mg | Calcium | 24 mg | Sugar | 7 g |

DIETARY EXCHANGES: 1 Lean Meat, ½ Fruit, 1 Vegetable

# SMOKED SALMON APPETIZERS

*Turn the classic combination of lox, bagels and cream cheese into an elegant opening for your holiday festivities. Lox is smoked salmon that has been brine-cured before smoking, resulting in a saltier taste; if you wish, ask for the less salty "Nova" lox.*

¼ cup reduced-fat or fat-free cream cheese, softened
1 tablespoon chopped fresh dill *or* 1 teaspoon dried dill weed

⅛ teaspoon ground red pepper
4 ounces thinly sliced smoked salmon or lox
24 melba toast rounds or other low-fat crackers

**1** Combine cream cheese, dill and pepper in small bowl; stir to blend. Spread evenly over each slice of salmon. Starting with short side, roll up salmon slices jelly-roll fashion. Place on plate; cover with plastic wrap. Chill at least 1 hour or up to 4 hours before serving.

**2** Using a sharp knife, cut salmon rolls crosswise into ¾-inch pieces. Place pieces, cut side down, on serving plate. Garnish each piece with dill sprig, if desired. Serve cold or at room temperature with melba rounds.

*Makes about 2 dozen appetizers
(3 appetizers per serving)*

**Nutrients per Serving:**

| Calories | 80 (21% calories from fat) | | | | |
|---|---|---|---|---|---|
| Total Fat | 2 g | Carbohydrate | 10 g | Iron | trace |
| Saturated Fat | 1 g | Dietary Fiber | 1 g | Vitamin A | 36 RE |
| Cholesterol | 6 mg | Protein | 6 g | Vitamin C | trace |
| Sodium | 241 mg | Calcium | 27 mg | Sugar | 0 g |

DIETARY EXCHANGES: ½ Starch/Bread, ½ Lean Meat

# SOUTHERN CRAB CAKES WITH RÉMOULADE DIPPING SAUCE

10 ounces fresh lump crabmeat
1½ cups fresh white or sourdough bread crumbs, divided
¼ cup chopped green onions
½ cup nonfat or reduced-fat mayonnaise, divided
2 tablespoons coarse grain or spicy brown mustard, divided

¾ teaspoon hot pepper sauce, divided
1 egg white, lightly beaten
2 teaspoons olive oil, divided
Lemon wedges

**1** Preheat oven to 200°F. Combine crabmeat, ¾ cup bread crumbs and green onions in medium bowl. Add ¼ cup mayonnaise, 1 tablespoon mustard, ½ teaspoon pepper sauce and egg white; mix well. Using ¼ cup mixture per cake, shape eight ½-inch-thick cakes. Roll crab cakes lightly in remaining ¾ cup bread crumbs.

**2** Heat large nonstick skillet over medium heat until hot; add 1 teaspoon oil. Add 4 crab cakes; cook 4 to 5 minutes per side or until golden brown. Transfer to serving platter; keep warm in oven. Repeat with remaining 1 teaspoon oil and crab cakes.

**3** To prepare dipping sauce, combine remaining ¼ cup mayonnaise, 1 tablespoon mustard and ¼ teaspoon pepper sauce in small bowl; mix well.

**4** Serve warm crab cakes with lemon wedges and dipping sauce.

*Makes 8 servings*

**Nutrients per Serving:**

| | | | | | |
|---|---|---|---|---|---|
| Calories | 81 (25% calories from fat) | | | | |
| Total Fat | 2 g | Carbohydrate | 8 g | Iron | 1 mg |
| Saturated Fat | trace | Dietary Fiber | trace | Vitamin A | 13 RE |
| Cholesterol | 30 mg | Protein | 7 g | Vitamin C | 1 mg |
| Sodium | 376 mg | Calcium | 48 mg | Sugar | trace |

DIETARY EXCHANGES: ½ Starch/Bread, 1 Lean Meat

# SHRIMP DIP WITH CRUDITÉS

*Any combination of raw vegetables, including broccoli, cauliflower or celery, can be added to this simple, yet elegant appetizer. Be sure to choose veggies of different colors and shapes to create an eye-catching display.*

1 can (6 ounces) cooked
   shrimp, drained, divided
½ cup reduced-fat cream
   cheese, softened
⅓ cup plus 1 tablespoon thinly
   sliced green onions, divided
3 tablespoons light or fat-free
   Caesar salad dressing
2 teaspoons prepared
   horseradish

¼ teaspoon salt
2 red or yellow bell peppers,
   cut into 2×1-inch pieces
4 large carrots, peeled,
   diagonally sliced ¼ inch
   thick
10 crispbread or other low-fat
   crackers

**1** Reserve several shrimp for garnish. Combine remaining shrimp, cream cheese, ⅓ cup green onions, salad dressing, horseradish and salt in medium bowl; mix well. Transfer to serving dish; top with reserved shrimp and remaining 1 tablespoon green onions. Cover and chill at least 30 minutes before serving.

**2** Serve with bell peppers, carrots and crackers.    *Makes 10 servings*

### Nutrients per Serving:

| Calories | 127 (29% calories from fat) | | | | |
|---|---|---|---|---|---|
| Total Fat | 4 g | Carbohydrate | 16 g | Iron | 1 mg |
| Saturated Fat | trace | Dietary Fiber | 2 g | Vitamin A | 1133 RE |
| Cholesterol | 37 mg | Protein | 7 g | Vitamin C | 106 mg |
| Sodium | 217 mg | Calcium | 41 mg | Sugar | 2 g |

DIETARY EXCHANGES: ½ Starch/Bread, ½ Lean Meat, 2 Vegetable, ½ Fat

# CRANBERRY-LIME MARGARITA PUNCH

*This refreshing and festive punch adds sparkle and panache to any occasion.*

6 cups water
1 container (12 ounces) frozen
   cranberry juice cocktail
½ cup lime juice

¼ cup sugar
2 cups ice cubes
1 cup ginger ale or tequila
1 lime, sliced

 Combine water, cranberry juice, lime juice and sugar in punch bowl; stir until sugar dissolves.

 Stir in ice cubes, ginger ale and lime; garnish with fresh cranberries, if desired.

*Makes 10 servings*

**Nutrients per Serving:**

| Calories | 97 (0% calories from fat) | | | | |
|---|---|---|---|---|---|
| Total Fat | trace | Carbohydrate | 25 g | Iron | trace |
| Saturated Fat | trace | Dietary Fiber | trace | Vitamin A | 1 RE |
| Cholesterol | 0 mg | Protein | trace | Vitamin C | 32 mg |
| Sodium | 3 mg | Calcium | 8 mg | Sugar | 7 g |

DIETARY EXCHANGES: 1½ Fruit

❖

### Cook's Tip

Add a festive touch to your holidays by adding a colorful and appealing ice ring to your punch bowl. Simply fill a ring mold with some punch and fresh cranberries, freeze until solid, unmold and float the ice ring in the punch bowl.

❖

# OREGON HOT APPLE CIDER

*To warm up those cold holiday nights, sit by the fire and sip this enticing classic direct from the Pacific Northwest. The pear provides an elegant touch.*

8 whole cloves
8 cups apple cider
½ cup dried cherries
½ cup dried cranberries

3 cinnamon sticks, broken in half
1 pear, quartered, cored, sliced

**1** Bundle cloves in small piece of cheesecloth. Tie cheesecloth to form small sack.

**2** Combine cider, cherries, cranberries, cinnamon and cheesecloth sack in large saucepan. Heat just to a simmer; do not boil. Remove cheese-cloth sack and discard.

**3** Add pear before serving.

*Makes 8 servings*

---

**Nutrients per Serving:**

| | | | | | | |
|---|---|---|---|---|---|---|
| Calories | 180 (3% calories from fat) | | | | | |
| Total Fat | 1 g | Carbohydrate | 48 g | Iron | 2 mg |
| Saturated Fat | trace | Dietary Fiber | 2 g | Vitamin A | 97 RE |
| Cholesterol | 0 mg | Protein | 1 g | Vitamin C | 13 mg |
| Sodium | 10 mg | Calcium | 31 mg | Sugar | 2 g |

DIETARY EXCHANGES: 3 Fruit

---

### Cook's Tip
To quickly ripen a pear, place it, along with an apple, in a paper bag. Poke a few holes in the bag with a knife and let the bag stand at room temperature.

# SALADS & SOUPS

## PEAR AND CRANBERRY SALAD

*Bring a touch of elegance to the holidays and create a medley of robust flavors. Be sure to use ripe pears; Forelles and Red Bartletts are particularly well suited for use in this salad. A high-quality balsamic vinegar is a wonderful addition to your pantry.*

½ cup canned whole berry
    cranberry sauce
2 tablespoons balsamic vinegar
1 tablespoon olive or canola oil
12 cups (9 ounces) packed
    assorted bitter or gourmet
    salad greens

6 small or 4 large pears (about
    1¾ pounds)
2 ounces blue or Gorgonzola
    cheese, crumbled
Freshly ground black pepper

**1** Combine cranberry sauce, vinegar and oil in small bowl; mix well. (Dressing may be covered and refrigerated up to 2 days before serving.)

**2** Arrange greens on six serving plates. Cut pears lengthwise into ½-inch-thick slices; cut core and seeds from each slice. Arrange pears attractively over greens. Drizzle cranberry dressing over pears and greens; sprinkle with cheese. Sprinkle with pepper to taste.

*Makes 6 servings*

### Nutrients per Serving:

| Calories | 161 (29% calories from fat) | | | | |
|---|---|---|---|---|---|
| Total Fat | 6 g | Carbohydrate | 26 g | Iron | 1 mg |
| Saturated Fat | 2 g | Dietary Fiber | 2 g | Vitamin A | 313 RE |
| Cholesterol | 7 mg | Protein | 4 g | Vitamin C | 20 mg |
| Sodium | 165 mg | Calcium | 122 mg | Sugar | 1 g |

DIETARY EXCHANGES: 2 Fruit, 1 Fat

# SPICY PUMPKIN SOUP WITH GREEN CHILI SWIRL

*Warm up the winter holidays with this Southwestern special featuring regional spices and the added kick of green chilies. Chilies may be rinsed in cold water before using to decrease spiciness.*

1 can (4 ounces) diced green chilies, drained
¼ cup reduced-fat sour cream
¼ cup fresh cilantro leaves
1 can (15 ounces) solid-pack pumpkin
1 can (about 14 ounces) fat-free reduced-sodium chicken broth

½ cup water
1 teaspoon ground cumin
½ teaspoon chili powder
¼ teaspoon garlic powder
⅛ teaspoon ground red pepper (optional)

**1** Combine green chilies, sour cream and cilantro in food processor or blender; process until smooth.*

**2** Combine pumpkin, chicken broth, water, cumin, chili powder, garlic powder and pepper, if desired, in medium saucepan; stir in ¼ cup green chili mixture. Bring to a boil; reduce heat to medium. Simmer, uncovered, 5 minutes, stirring occasionally.

**3** Pour into serving bowls. Top each serving with small dollops of remaining green chili mixture and additional sour cream, if desired. Run tip of spoon through dollops to swirl.    *Makes 4 servings*

*Omit food processor step by adding green chilies directly to soup. Finely chop cilantro and combine with sour cream. Dollop with sour cream mixture as directed.

### Nutrients per Serving:

| Calories | 72 (17% calories from fat) | | | | |
|---|---|---|---|---|---|
| Total Fat | 1 g | Carbohydrate | 12 g | Iron | 2 mg |
| Saturated Fat | trace | Dietary Fiber | 4 g | Vitamin A | 2424 RE |
| Cholesterol | 5 mg | Protein | 4 g | Vitamin C | 5 mg |
| Sodium | 276 mg | Calcium | 57 mg | Sugar | 0 g |

DIETARY EXCHANGES: 1 Starch/Bread

# CRAB COBB SALAD

*Fresh or pasteurized crabmeat can be substituted for the canned variety. Crabmeat should always smell fresh and sweet; lump and backfin meat are the best kinds.*

12 cups washed and torn
    romaine lettuce
2 cans (6 ounces each)
    crabmeat, drained
2 cups diced ripe tomatoes or
    halved cherry tomatoes
¼ cup (1½ ounces) crumbled
    blue or Gorgonzola cheese

¼ cup cholesterol-free bacon
    bits
¾ cup fat-free Italian or Caesar
    salad dressing
Freshly ground black pepper

 Cover large serving platter with lettuce. Arrange crabmeat, tomatoes, blue cheese and bacon bits attractively over lettuce.

 Just before serving, drizzle dressing evenly over salad; toss well. Transfer to 8 chilled serving plates; sprinkle with pepper to taste.

*Makes 8 servings*

**Nutrients per Serving:**

| | | | | | | |
|---|---|---|---|---|---|---|
| Calories | 110 (27% calories from fat) | | | | | |
| Total Fat | 3 g | Carbohydrate | 8 g | Iron | 2 mg |
| Saturated Fat | 1 g | Dietary Fiber | 2 g | Vitamin A | 262 RE |
| Cholesterol | 46 mg | Protein | 12 g | Vitamin C | 31 mg |
| Sodium | 666 mg | Calcium | 75 mg | Sugar | 3 g |

DIETARY EXCHANGES: 1½ Lean Meat, 1½ Vegetable

❖

## Cook's Tip

This salad can be covered and refrigerated up to five hours before serving. Toss with dressing immediately before serving.

❖

# TEXAS-STYLE CHILI

*Called a "bowl of red" deep in the heart of Texas, this chili is usually served with the beans on the side. For those who like their chili with a bit more fire, use a hotter salsa or even a few dashes of hot pepper sauce. This dish is even better when it's prepared a day ahead, chilled and brought back to a simmer before serving.*

Nonstick cooking spray
1 pound lean boneless beef chuck, cut into ½-inch pieces
2 cups chopped onions
5 cloves garlic, minced
2 tablespoons chili powder
1 tablespoon ground cumin
1 teaspoon ground coriander
1 teaspoon dried oregano leaves or ground oregano

2½ cups fat-free reduced-sodium beef broth
1 cup prepared salsa or picante sauce
2 cans (16 ounces each) pinto or red beans (or one of each), rinsed and drained
½ cup chopped fresh cilantro
½ cup nonfat sour cream
1 cup chopped ripe tomatoes

**1** Spray Dutch oven or large saucepan with nonstick cooking spray; heat over medium-high heat until hot. Add beef, onions and garlic; cook and stir until beef is no longer pink, about 5 minutes. Sprinkle mixture with chili powder, cumin, coriander and oregano; mix well. Add beef broth and salsa; bring to a boil. Cover; simmer 45 minutes.

**2** Stir in beans; continue to simmer uncovered 30 minutes or until beef is tender and chili has thickened, stirring occasionally.

**3** Stir in cilantro. Ladle into bowls; top with sour cream and tomatoes. Garnish with pickled jalapeño peppers, if desired.      *Makes 8 servings*

### Nutrients per Serving:

| | | | | | | |
|---|---|---|---|---|---|---|
| Calories | 268 (21% calories from fat) | | | | | |
| Total Fat | 7 g | Carbohydrate | 31 g | Iron | 3 mg |
| Saturated Fat | 2 g | Dietary Fiber | 2 g | Vitamin A | 194 RE |
| Cholesterol | 37 mg | Protein | 25 g | Vitamin C | 21 mg |
| Sodium | 725 mg | Calcium | 62 mg | Sugar | 2 g |

DIETARY EXCHANGES: 1½ Starch/Bread, 2½ Lean Meat, 1 Vegetable

# DOUBLE CORN & CHEDDAR CHOWDER

*You'll swear you're in the heartland of the Midwest when you indulge in this soup—it's so rich and creamy your family and friends won't believe it's low in fat and cholesterol. Replace some of the chicken broth with light beer to produce a truly authentic Wisconsin specialty.*

1 tablespoon margarine
1 cup chopped onion
2 tablespoons all-purpose flour
2½ cups fat-free reduced-sodium chicken broth
1 can (16 ounces) cream-style corn
1 cup frozen whole kernel corn

½ cup finely diced red bell pepper
½ teaspoon hot pepper sauce
¾ cup (3 ounces) shredded sharp Cheddar cheese
Freshly ground black pepper (optional)

**1** Melt margarine in large saucepan over medium heat. Add onion; cook and stir 5 minutes. Sprinkle onion with flour; cook and stir 1 minute.

**2** Add chicken broth; bring to a boil, stirring frequently. Add cream-style corn, corn kernels, bell pepper and pepper sauce; bring to a simmer. Cover; simmer 15 minutes.

**3** Remove from heat; gradually stir in cheese until melted. Ladle into soup bowls; sprinkle with black pepper, if desired.    *Makes 6 servings*

**Double Corn, Cheddar & Rice Chowder:** Add 1 cup cooked white or brown rice with corn.

### Nutrients per Serving:

| Calories | 180 (28% calories from fat) | | | | |
|---|---|---|---|---|---|
| Total Fat | 6 g | Carbohydrate | 28 g | Iron | 1 mg |
| Saturated Fat | 2 g | Dietary Fiber | 2 g | Vitamin A | 177 RE |
| Cholesterol | 10 mg | Protein | 7 g | Vitamin C | 49 mg |
| Sodium | 498 mg | Calcium | 88 mg | Sugar | 1 g |

DIETARY EXCHANGES: 1½ Starch/Bread, ½ Lean Meat, 1 Fat

# SANTA FE GRILLED VEGETABLE SALAD

*Nothing beats the flavor of food off the grill, especially if the marinade is as robust as this citrus-enhanced Southwestern fare. You may want to peel the eggplant after grilling, as the skin may be slightly bitter.*

1 medium yellow summer squash, cut into halves

1 medium zucchini, cut into halves

1 green bell pepper, cut into quarters

1 red bell pepper, cut into quarters

2 baby eggplants (6 ounces each), cut into halves

1 small onion, peeled, cut into halves

½ cup orange juice

2 tablespoons lime juice

1 tablespoon olive oil

2 cloves garlic, minced

1 teaspoon dried oregano leaves

¼ teaspoon salt

¼ teaspoon ground red pepper

¼ teaspoon ground black pepper

2 tablespoons chopped fresh cilantro

**1** Combine all ingredients except cilantro in large bowl; toss to coat.

**2** To prevent sticking, spray grid with nonstick cooking spray. Prepare coals for grilling. Place vegetables on grid, 2 to 3 inches from hot coals; reserve marinade. Grill 3 to 4 minutes per side or until tender and lightly charred; cool 10 minutes. Or, place vegetables on rack of broiler pan coated with nonstick cooking spray; reserve marinade. Broil 2 to 3 inches from heat, 3 to 4 minutes per side or until tender; cool 10 minutes.

**3** Remove peel from eggplants, if desired. Slice vegetables into bite-sized pieces; return to reserved marinade. Stir in cilantro; toss to coat.

*Makes 8 servings*

**Nutrients per Serving:**

| Calories | 63 (27% calories from fat) | | | | |
|---|---|---|---|---|---|
| Total Fat | 2 g | Carbohydrate | 11 g | Iron | 1 mg |
| Saturated Fat | trace | Dietary Fiber | 1 g | Vitamin A | 210 RE |
| Cholesterol | 0 mg | Protein | 2 g | Vitamin C | 85 mg |
| Sodium | 70 mg | Calcium | 27 mg | Sugar | 2 g |

DIETARY EXCHANGES: 2 Vegetable, ½ Fat

# SPINACH SALAD WITH HOT APPLE DRESSING

*Even though green leafy vegetables, like spinach, are some of the healthiest foods you can eat, it used to be difficult to make them appealing and tempting—until now! Turkey bacon offers all the flavor of regular bacon with nearly half the saturated fat.*

6 strips turkey bacon
¾ cup apple cider
2 tablespoons brown sugar
4 teaspoons rice wine vinegar
¼ teaspoon ground black pepper
6 cups washed and torn spinach
  leaves

2 cups sliced mushrooms
1 medium tomato, cut into
  wedges
½ cup thinly sliced red onion

**1** Heat medium nonstick skillet over medium heat until hot; add bacon and cook 2 to 3 minutes per side or until crisp; remove from pan. Coarsely chop 3 pieces; set aside. Finely chop remaining 3 pieces; return to skillet. Add apple cider, sugar, vinegar and pepper. Heat just to a simmer; remove from heat.

**2** Combine spinach, mushrooms, tomato and onion in large bowl. Add dressing; toss to coat. Top with reserved bacon.          *Makes 6 servings*

**Nutrients per Serving:**

| Calories | 95 (28% calories from fat) | | | | |
|---|---|---|---|---|---|
| Total Fat | 3 g | Carbohydrate | 14 g | Iron | 2 mg |
| Saturated Fat | 1 g | Dietary Fiber | 2 g | Vitamin A | 389 RE |
| Cholesterol | 9 mg | Protein | 5 g | Vitamin C | 22 mg |
| Sodium | 256 mg | Calcium | 74 mg | Sugar | 1 g |

DIETARY EXCHANGES: ½ Fruit, 1½ Vegetable, ½ Fat

# NEW ENGLAND CLAM CHOWDER

*The word "chowder" comes from the French word* chaudière, *the stew pot in which fishermen cooked their catches of the day. The New England version features milk, while the Manhattan (or red) variety adds tomatoes to the basic recipe.*

| | |
|---|---|
| 1 can (5 ounces) whole baby clams, undrained | ⅔ cup evaporated skimmed milk |
| 1 baking potato, peeled, coarsely chopped | ¼ teaspoon ground white pepper |
| ¼ cup finely chopped onion | ¼ teaspoon dried thyme leaves |
| | 1 tablespoon reduced-calorie margarine |

**1** Drain clams; reserve juice. Add enough water to reserved juice to measure ⅔ cup. Combine clam juice mixture, potato and onion in medium saucepan. Bring to a boil over high heat; reduce heat and simmer 8 minutes or until potato is tender.

**2** Add milk, pepper and thyme to saucepan. Increase heat to medium-high. Cook and stir 2 minutes. Add margarine. Cook 5 minutes or until chowder thickens, stirring occasionally.

**3** Add clams; cook and stir 5 minutes or until clams are firm.

*Makes 2 servings*

### Nutrients per Serving:

| | | | | | |
|---|---|---|---|---|---|
| Calories | 191 (18% calories from fat) | | | | |
| Total Fat | 4 g | Carbohydrate | 27 g | Iron | 4 mg |
| Saturated Fat | 1 g | Dietary Fiber | 1 g | Vitamin A | 164 RE |
| Cholesterol | 47 mg | Protein | 14 g | Vitamin C | 7 mg |
| Sodium | 205 mg | Calcium | 298 mg | Sugar | 2 g |

DIETARY EXCHANGES: 1 Starch/Bread, 1 Lean Meat, 1 Milk

# MAIN DISHES

## TURKEY & PASTA WITH CILANTRO PESTO

*A member of the parsley family, cilantro (also known as coriander leaves) is the world's most widely used herb. Its vibrant flavor infuses this pasta and turkey combination with a Southwestern sensation. Turkey breast cut into strips may be substituted for turkey tenders.*

1 pound turkey tenders, cut into strips
3 cloves garlic, minced
½ teaspoon ground cumin
¼ teaspoon ground red pepper
¼ teaspoon ground black pepper
2 tablespoons olive oil
1½ cups chopped seeded tomatoes
½ cup chopped fresh cilantro
¼ cup (1 ounce) grated Parmesan cheese
2 tablespoons orange juice
12 ounces dry linguine, cooked and kept warm

**1** Combine turkey, garlic, cumin, red pepper and black pepper in medium bowl; toss to coat. Heat oil in large skillet over medium-high heat. Add turkey mixture; cook 4 to 6 minutes or until turkey is no longer pink in center.

**2** Add tomatoes; cook 2 minutes. Stir in cilantro, cheese and orange juice; cook 1 minute.

**3** Toss turkey mixture and linguine in large bowl. Serve immediately.

*Makes 6 servings*

### Nutrients per Serving:

| Calories | 365 (22% calories from fat) | | | | |
|---|---|---|---|---|---|
| Total Fat | 9 g | Carbohydrate | 48 g | Iron | 3 mg |
| Saturated Fat | 2 g | Dietary Fiber | 1 g | Vitamin A | 62 RE |
| Cholesterol | 33 mg | Protein | 23 g | Vitamin C | 14 mg |
| Sodium | 112 mg | Calcium | 91 mg | Sugar | 2 g |

DIETARY EXCHANGES: 3 Starch/Bread, 1½ Lean Meat, 1 Vegetable, 1 Fat

# ROAST TURKEY WITH CRANBERRY STUFFING

*A New England twist enlivens this quintessential holiday dish.
Taking off the turkey skin eliminates loads of fat without removing
any of the succulence.*

Cranberry Stuffing (page 44)  1 turkey (8 to 10 pounds)

**1** Prepare Cranberry Stuffing. *Reduce oven temperature to 350°F.*

**2** Remove giblets from turkey. Rinse turkey and cavity in cold water;
pat dry with paper towels. Fill turkey cavity loosely with stuffing. Place
remaining stuffing in casserole sprayed with nonstick cooking spray.
Cover casserole; refrigerate until baking time.

**3** Spray roasting pan with nonstick cooking spray. Place turkey, breast
side up, on rack in roasting pan. Bake 3 hours or until thermometer
inserted in thickest part of thigh registers 185°F and juices run clear.

**4** Transfer turkey to serving platter. Cover loosely with foil; let stand
20 minutes. Place covered casserole of stuffing in oven; *increase oven
temperature to 375°F.* Bake 25 to 30 minutes or until hot.

**5** Remove and discard turkey skin. Slice turkey and serve with
Cranberry Stuffing and Spicy Southwestern Vegetable Sauté (page 66),
if desired. Garnish with fresh rosemary sprigs, if desired.

*Makes 10 servings*

*continued on page 44*

*Roast Turkey with Cranberry Stuffing, continued*

## CRANBERRY STUFFING

1 loaf (12 ounces) Italian or
    French bread, cut into
    ½-inch cubes
2 tablespoons margarine
1½ cups chopped onions
1½ cups chopped celery
2 teaspoons poultry seasoning
1 teaspoon dried thyme leaves

½ teaspoon dried rosemary
¼ teaspoon salt
¼ teaspoon ground black pepper
1 cup coarsely chopped fresh
    cranberries
1 tablespoon sugar
¾ cup fat-free reduced-sodium
    chicken broth

**1** Preheat oven to 375°F. Arrange bread on two 15×10-inch jelly-roll pans. Bake 12 minutes or until lightly toasted.

**2** Melt margarine in large saucepan over medium heat. Add onions and celery. Cook and stir 8 minutes or until vegetables are tender; remove from heat. Add bread cubes, poultry seasoning, thyme, rosemary, salt and pepper; mix well. Combine cranberries and sugar in small bowl; mix well. Add to bread mixture; toss well. Drizzle chicken broth evenly over mixture; toss well. *Makes 10 servings*

### Nutrients per Serving:
*(turkey and stuffing)*

| | | | | | | |
|---|---|---|---|---|---|---|
| Calories | 439 (26% calories from fat) | | | | | |
| Total Fat | 12 g | Carbohydrate | 23 g | Iron | 5 mg |
| Saturated Fat | 4 g | Dietary Fiber | 1 g | Vitamin A | 32 RE |
| Cholesterol | 136 mg | Protein | 56 g | Vitamin C | 4 mg |
| Sodium | 445 mg | Calcium | 91 mg | Sugar | 2 g |

DIETARY EXCHANGES: 1½ Starch/Bread, 6 Lean Meat

# OVEN-ROASTED BOSTON SCROD

*Scrod, another name for young cod, was introduced at the Parker House Hotel in Boston in the 1890's. Scrod's naturally delicate flavor and flaky texture dominate this easy-to-prepare dish.*

½ cup seasoned dry bread
    crumbs
1 teaspoon grated fresh lemon
    peel
1 teaspoon dried dill weed
1 teaspoon paprika
3 tablespoons all-purpose flour
2 egg whites

1 tablespoon water
1½ pounds Boston scrod or
    orange roughy fillets, cut
    into 6 (4-ounce) pieces
2 tablespoons margarine,
    melted
Tartar Sauce (page 46)
Lemon wedges

**1** Preheat oven to 400°F. Spray 15×10-inch jelly-roll pan with nonstick cooking spray. Combine bread crumbs, lemon peel, dill and paprika in shallow bowl or pie plate. Place flour in resealable plastic food storage bag. Beat egg whites and water together in another shallow bowl or pie plate.

**2** Add fish, one fillet at a time, to bag. Seal bag; turn to coat fish lightly. Dip fish into egg white mixture, letting excess drip off. Roll fish in bread crumb mixture. Place in prepared jelly-roll pan. Repeat with remaining fish fillets. Brush margarine evenly over fish. Bake 15 to 18 minutes or until fish begins to flake when tested with fork.

**3** Prepare Tartar Sauce while fish is baking. Serve fish with lemon wedges and Tartar Sauce. *Makes 6 servings*

*continued on page 46*

*Oven-Roasted Boston Scrod, continued*

## TARTAR SAUCE

½ cup nonfat or reduced-fat
   mayonnaise

¼ cup sweet pickle relish

2 teaspoons Dijon mustard

¼ teaspoon hot pepper sauce
   (optional)

 Combine all ingredients in small bowl; mix well.

*Makes ⅔ cup*

**Nutrients per Serving:**

| | | | | | |
|---|---|---|---|---|---|
| Calories | 215 (21% calories from fat) | | | | |
| Total Fat | 5 g | Carbohydrate | 18 g | Iron | 1 mg |
| Saturated Fat | 1 g | Dietary Fiber | trace | Vitamin A | 81 RE |
| Cholesterol | 49 mg | Protein | 23 g | Vitamin C | 2 mg |
| Sodium | 754 mg | Calcium | 31 mg | Sugar | trace |

DIETARY EXCHANGES: 1 Starch/Bread, 2½ Lean Meat

## Health Note

Scrod and cod are naturally low in fat and calories and
high in valuable omega-3 fatty acids.

# SHRIMP ÉTOUFFÉE

*The classic Cajun comfort food, étouffée literally means "to smother." This version eliminates most of the fat, but still "smothers" your tastebuds with abundant flavor and spice.*

3 tablespoons vegetable oil
¼ cup all-purpose flour
1 cup chopped onion
1 cup chopped green bell pepper
½ cup chopped carrots
½ cup chopped celery
4 cloves garlic, minced
1 can (about 14 ounces) clear vegetable broth
1 bottle (8 ounces) clam juice
½ teaspoon salt
2½ pounds large shrimp, peeled and deveined
1 teaspoon crushed red pepper
1 teaspoon hot pepper sauce
4 cups hot cooked white or basmati rice
½ cup chopped flat leaf parsley

**1** Heat oil in Dutch oven over medium heat. Add flour; cook and stir 10 to 15 minutes or until flour mixture is deep golden brown. Add onion, bell pepper, carrots, celery and garlic; cook and stir 5 minutes.

**2** Stir in vegetable broth, clam juice and salt; bring to a boil. Simmer, uncovered, 10 minutes or until vegetables are tender. Stir in shrimp, red pepper and pepper sauce; simmer 6 to 8 minutes or until shrimp are opaque.

**3** Ladle into eight shallow bowls; top each with ½ cup rice. Sprinkle with parsley. Serve with additional pepper sauce, if desired.

*Makes 8 servings*

**Nutrients per Serving:**

| | | | | | | |
|---|---|---|---|---|---|---|
| Calories | 306 (20% calories from fat) | | | | | |
| Total Fat | 7 g | Carbohydrate | 32 g | Iron | 5 mg |
| Saturated Fat | 1 g | Dietary Fiber | 1 g | Vitamin A | 401 RE |
| Cholesterol | 219 mg | Protein | 27 g | Vitamin C | 36 mg |
| Sodium | 454 mg | Calcium | 72 mg | Sugar | 2 g |

DIETARY EXCHANGES: 1½ Starch/Bread, 3 Lean Meat, 1 Vegetable

# HOPPIN' JOHN SUPPER

*The traditional good luck New Year's Day feast in the South, hoppin' John is brimming with flavor and perfect for holiday festivities.*

1 cup uncooked converted white rice

1 can (about 14 ounces) fat-free reduced-sodium chicken broth

¼ cup water

1 package (16 ounces) frozen black-eyed peas, thawed

1 tablespoon vegetable oil

1 cup chopped onion

1 cup diced carrots

¾ cup thinly sliced celery with tops

3 cloves garlic, minced

12 ounces reduced-sodium lean fully cooked ham, cut into ¾-inch pieces

¾ teaspoon hot pepper sauce

½ teaspoon salt

**1** Combine rice, chicken broth and water in large saucepan; bring to a boil over high heat. Reduce heat; cover and simmer 10 minutes. Stir in black-eyed peas; cover and simmer 10 minutes or until rice and peas are tender and liquid is absorbed.

**2** Meanwhile, heat oil in large skillet over medium heat. Add onion, carrots, celery and garlic; cook and stir 15 minutes or until vegetables are tender. Add ham; heat through. Add hot rice mixture, pepper sauce and salt; mix well. Cover; cook over low heat 10 minutes. Sprinkle with parsley and serve with additional pepper sauce, if desired.

*Makes 8 servings*

**Nutrients per Serving:**

| | | | | | | |
|---|---|---|---|---|---|---|
| Calories | 245 (13% calories from fat) | | | | | |
| Total Fat | 3 g | Carbohydrate | 38 g | Iron | 3 mg |
| Saturated Fat | 1 g | Dietary Fiber | 4 g | Vitamin A | 393 RE |
| Cholesterol | 20 mg | Protein | 16 g | Vitamin C | 6 mg |
| Sodium | 624 mg | Calcium | 42 mg | Sugar | 3 g |

DIETARY EXCHANGES: 2 Starch/Bread, 1 Lean Meat, 1½ Vegetable

# MUSTARD-CRUSTED ROAST PORK

3 tablespoons Dijon mustard
4 teaspoons minced garlic, divided
2 whole well-trimmed pork tenderloins, about 1 pound each
2 tablespoons dried thyme
1 teaspoon ground black pepper
½ teaspoon salt

1 pound asparagus spears, ends trimmed
2 red or yellow bell peppers (or one of each), cut lengthwise into ½-inch-wide strips
1 cup fat-free reduced-sodium chicken broth, divided

**1** Preheat oven to 375°F. Combine mustard and 3 teaspoons garlic in small bowl. Spread mustard mixture evenly over top and sides of both tenderloins. Combine thyme, black pepper and salt in small bowl; reserve 1 teaspoon mixture. Sprinkle remaining mixture evenly over tenderloins, patting so that seasoning adheres to mustard. Place tenderloins on rack in shallow roasting pan. Roast 25 minutes.

**2** Arrange asparagus and bell peppers in single layer in shallow casserole or 13×9-inch baking pan. Add ¼ cup broth, reserved thyme mixture and remaining 1 teaspoon garlic; toss to coat.

**3** Roast vegetables in oven alongside tenderloins 15 to 20 minutes or until thermometer inserted into center of pork registers 160°F and vegetables are tender. Transfer tenderloins to carving board; tent with foil and let stand 5 minutes. Arrange vegetables on serving platter, reserving juices in dish; cover and keep warm. Add remaining ¾ cup broth and juices in dish to roasting pan. Place over range top burner(s); simmer 3 to 4 minutes over medium-high heat or until juices are reduced to ¾ cup, stirring frequently. Carve tenderloins crosswise into ¼-inch slices; arrange on serving platter. Spoon juices over pork and vegetables.

*Makes 8 servings*

### Nutrients per Serving:

| | | | | | |
|---|---|---|---|---|---|
| Calories | 182 (23% calories from fat) | | | | |
| Total Fat | 5 g | Carbohydrate | 8 g | Iron | 4 mg |
| Saturated Fat | 2 g | Dietary Fiber | 1 g | Vitamin A | 392 RE |
| Cholesterol | 65 mg | Protein | 27 g | Vitamin C | 134 mg |
| Sodium | 304 mg | Calcium | 55 mg | Sugar | trace |

DIETARY EXCHANGES: 3 Lean Meat, 1 Vegetable

# HAZELNUT-COATED SALMON STEAKS

*In the United States, hazelnuts (also called filberts) are grown almost exclusively in Oregon, and a single tree will yield nuts for hundreds of years. The skins are bitter, so it is best to remove them.*

¼ cup hazelnuts
4 salmon steaks, about 5 ounces each
1 tablespoon apple butter

1 tablespoon Dijon mustard
¼ teaspoon dried thyme leaves
⅛ teaspoon ground black pepper
2 cups cooked white rice

**1** Preheat oven to 375°F. Place hazelnuts on baking sheet; bake 8 minutes or until lightly browned. Quickly transfer nuts to clean dry dish towel. Fold towel; rub vigorously to remove as much of the skins as possible. Finely chop hazelnuts using food processor, nut grinder or chef's knife.

**2** *Increase oven temperature to 450°F.* Place salmon in baking dish. Combine apple butter, mustard, thyme and pepper in small bowl. Brush on salmon; top each steak with nuts. Bake 14 to 16 minutes or until salmon flakes easily with fork. Serve with rice and steamed snow peas, if desired.

*Makes 4 servings*

**Nutrients per Serving:**

| Calories | 329 (30% calories from fat) | | | | |
|---|---|---|---|---|---|
| Total Fat | 11 g | Carbohydrate | 26 g | Iron | 3 mg |
| Saturated Fat | 1 g | Dietary Fiber | 1 g | Vitamin A | 45 RE |
| Cholesterol | 72 mg | Protein | 31 g | Vitamin C | trace |
| Sodium | 143 mg | Calcium | 34 mg | Sugar | trace |

DIETARY EXCHANGES: 1½ Starch/Bread, 4 Lean Meat

## Health Note

Salmon is one of the richest sources of omega-3 fatty acids. Evidence suggests that these acids may prevent blood clots, lessen arthritis pain and help treat the skin disorder psoriasis.

# EASY BRUNCH FRITTATA

*This Italian omelet is an ideal alternative to quiche
for your next brunch.*

1 cup small broccoli flowerets
2½ cups (12 ounces) frozen hash
    brown potatoes with onions
    and peppers (O'Brien style),
    thawed
1½ cups cholesterol-free egg
    substitute, thawed

2 tablespoons 2% low-fat milk
¾ teaspoon salt
¼ teaspoon ground black pepper
½ cup (2 ounces) shredded
    reduced-fat Cheddar cheese

**1** Preheat oven to 450°F. Coat medium nonstick ovenproof skillet with nonstick cooking spray. Heat skillet over medium heat until hot. Add broccoli; cook and stir 2 minutes. Add potatoes; cook and stir 5 minutes.

**2** Beat together egg substitute, milk, salt and pepper in small bowl; pour over potato mixture. Cook 5 minutes or until edges are set (center will still be wet).

**3** Transfer skillet to oven; bake 6 minutes or until center is set. Sprinkle with cheese; let stand 2 to 3 minutes or until cheese is melted.

**4** Cut into wedges; serve with low-fat sour cream, if desired.

*Makes 6 servings*

**Nutrients per Serving:**

| Calories | 102 (20% calories from fat) | | | | |
|---|---|---|---|---|---|
| Total Fat | 2 g | Carbohydrate | 11 g | Iron | 2 mg |
| Saturated Fat | 1 g | Dietary Fiber | 1 g | Vitamin A | 135 RE |
| Cholesterol | 7 mg | Protein | 9 g | Vitamin C | 23 mg |
| Sodium | 627 mg | Calcium | 124 mg | Sugar | 1 g |

DIETARY EXCHANGES: ½ Starch/Bread, 1 Lean Meat

# SIDE DISHES

## SOUTHERN-STYLE SUCCOTASH

*Taken from the Indian word meaning "boiled whole kernels of corn," succotash is a true favorite of the South. Hominy, corn kernels that have had their germ and hulls removed, is readily available in most supermarkets; it is high in calcium and B vitamins.*

2 tablespoons margarine
1 cup chopped onion
1 package (10 ounces) frozen
    lima beans, thawed
1 cup frozen whole corn
    kernels, thawed
½ cup chopped red bell pepper
1 can (15 to 16 ounces) hominy,
    drained

⅓ cup fat-free reduced-sodium
    chicken broth
½ teaspoon salt
¼ teaspoon hot pepper sauce
¼ cup chopped green onion tops
    or chives

**1** Melt margarine in large nonstick skillet over medium heat. Add onion; cook and stir 5 minutes. Add lima beans, corn and bell pepper. Cook and stir 5 minutes.

**2** Add hominy, chicken broth, salt and pepper sauce; simmer 5 minutes or until most of liquid has evaporated. Remove from heat; stir in green onions. Serve with Festive Cornmeal Biscuits (page 68), if desired.

*Makes 6 servings*

### Nutrients per Serving:

| | | | | | | |
|---|---|---|---|---|---|---|
| Calories | 175 (23% calories from fat) | | | | | |
| Total Fat | 5 g | Carbohydrate | 29 g | Iron | 2 mg |
| Saturated Fat | 1 g | Dietary Fiber | 5 g | Vitamin A | 197 RE |
| Cholesterol | 0 mg | Protein | 6 g | Vitamin C | 48 mg |
| Sodium | 406 mg | Calcium | 33 mg | Sugar | 3 g |

DIETARY EXCHANGES: 2 Starch/Bread, 1 Fat

# SPIRITED SWEET POTATO CASSEROLE

*Sweet potatoes were introduced to the South by Africans and have become synonymous with "Southern cooking." High in vitamins C and A, sweet potatoes are available year-round.*

2½ pounds sweet potatoes
2 tablespoons reduced-calorie margarine
⅓ cup 1% low-fat or skim milk
¼ cup packed brown sugar
2 tablespoons bourbon or apple juice

1 teaspoon ground cinnamon
1 teaspoon vanilla
2 egg whites
½ teaspoon salt
⅓ cup chopped pecans

**1** Preheat oven to 375°F. Bake potatoes 50 to 60 minutes or until very tender. Cool 10 minutes; leave oven on. Scoop pulp from warm potatoes into large bowl; discard potato skins. Add margarine to bowl; mash with potato masher until potatoes are fairly smooth and margarine has melted. Stir in milk, brown sugar, bourbon, cinnamon and vanilla; mix well.

**2** Beat egg whites with electric mixer at high speed until soft peaks form. Add salt; beat until stiff peaks form. Fold egg whites into sweet potato mixture.

**3** Spray 1½-quart soufflé dish with nonstick cooking spray. Spoon sweet potato mixture into dish; top with pecans.

**4** Bake 30 to 35 minutes or until casserole is puffed and pecans are toasted. Serve immediately. *Makes 8 servings*

**Nutrients per Serving:**

| Calories | 203 (21% calories from fat) | | | | |
|---|---|---|---|---|---|
| Total Fat | 5 g | Carbohydrate | 35 g | Iron | 1 mg |
| Saturated Fat | 1 g | Dietary Fiber | trace | Vitamin A | 1923 RE |
| Cholesterol | trace | Protein | 3 g | Vitamin C | 19 mg |
| Sodium | 202 mg | Calcium | 48 mg | Sugar | 1 g |

DIETARY EXCHANGES: 2 Starch/Bread, 1½ Fat

# POTATO PANCAKES WITH APPLE-CHERRY CHUTNEY

Apple-Cherry Chutney (recipe follows)
1 pound baking potatoes, about 2 medium
½ small onion
3 egg whites

2 tablespoons all-purpose flour
½ teaspoon salt
¼ teaspoon ground black pepper
4 teaspoons vegetable oil, divided

**1** Prepare Apple-Cherry Chutney; set aside.

**2** Peel potatoes; cut into chunks. Combine potatoes, onion, egg whites, flour, salt and pepper in food processor or blender; process until almost smooth (mixture will appear grainy).

**3** Heat large nonstick skillet 1 minute over medium heat. Add 1 teaspoon oil. Spoon 2 tablespoons batter per pancake into skillet. Cook 3 pancakes at a time, 3 minutes per side or until golden brown. Repeat with remaining batter, adding 1 teaspoon oil with each batch. Serve with Apple-Cherry Chutney.

*Makes 1 dozen pancakes (2 pancakes per serving)*

## APPLE–CHERRY CHUTNEY

1 cup chunky applesauce
½ cup canned tart cherries, drained
2 tablespoons brown sugar

1 teaspoon lemon juice
½ teaspoon ground cinnamon
⅛ teaspoon ground nutmeg

**1** Combine all ingredients in small saucepan; bring to a boil. Reduce heat; simmer 5 minutes. Serve warm.    *Makes 1½ cups*

### Nutrients per Serving:

| Calories | 164 (17% calories from fat) | | | | |
|---|---|---|---|---|---|
| Total Fat | 3 g | Carbohydrate | 31 g | Iron | 1 mg |
| Saturated Fat | trace | Dietary Fiber | 1 g | Vitamin A | 17 RE |
| Cholesterol | 0 mg | Protein | 4 g | Vitamin C | 12 mg |
| Sodium | 214 mg | Calcium | 18 mg | Sugar | 2 g |

DIETARY EXCHANGES: 1½ Starch/Bread, ½ Fruit, ½ Fat

# WILD & BROWN RICE WITH EXOTIC MUSHROOMS

1⅔ cups packaged unseasoned
    wild & brown rice blend
  6 cups water
½ ounce dried porcini or morel
    mushrooms
¾ cup boiling water
  2 tablespoons margarine
  8 ounces cremini (brown) or
    button mushrooms, sliced

2 cloves garlic, minced
2 tablespoons chopped fresh
    thyme *or* 2 teaspoons dried
    thyme leaves
1 teaspoon salt
¼ teaspoon ground black pepper
½ cup sliced green onions

**1** Combine rice and water in large saucepan; bring to a boil over high heat. Cover; simmer over low heat until rice is tender (check package for cooking time). Drain, but do not rinse.*

**2** Meanwhile, combine porcini mushrooms and boiling water in small bowl; let stand 30 minutes or until mushrooms are tender. Drain mushrooms, reserving liquid. Chop mushrooms; set aside.

**3** Melt margarine in large, deep skillet over medium heat. Add cremini mushrooms and garlic; cook and stir 5 minutes. Sprinkle thyme, salt and pepper over mushrooms; cook and stir 1 minute or until mushrooms are tender.

**4** Stir drained rice, porcini mushrooms and reserved mushroom liquid into skillet; cook and stir over medium-low heat 5 minutes or until hot. Stir in green onions. *Makes 8 servings*

*Rice may be prepared up to 3 hours before serving and kept covered at room temperature until it is added to fresh mushroom mixture.

**Nutrients per Serving:**

| Calories | 175 (21% calories from fat) | | | | |
|---|---|---|---|---|---|
| Total Fat | 4 g | Carbohydrate | 30 g | Iron | 1 mg |
| Saturated Fat | 1 g | Dietary Fiber | 2 g | Vitamin A | 61 RE |
| Cholesterol | 0 mg | Protein | 5 g | Vitamin C | 1 mg |
| Sodium | 304 mg | Calcium | 23 mg | Sugar | 1 g |

DIETARY EXCHANGES: 2 Starch/Bread, 1 Fat

# SPICY SOUTHWESTERN VEGETABLE SAUTÉ

*The staples of Southwestern cuisine are featured in this mélange of spice and savor. Adding more jalapeño peppers will certainly indulge those with a "fiery" palate.*

1 bag (16 ounces) frozen green beans
2 tablespoons water
1 tablespoon olive oil
1 red bell pepper, chopped
1 medium yellow summer squash or zucchini, chopped
1 jalapeño pepper, seeded, chopped*

½ teaspoon garlic powder
½ teaspoon ground cumin
½ teaspoon chili powder
¼ cup sliced green onions
2 tablespoons chopped fresh cilantro (optional)
1 tablespoon brown sugar

**1** Heat large skillet over medium heat; add green beans, water and oil. Cover; cook 4 minutes, stirring occasionally.

**2** Add bell pepper, squash, jalapeño, garlic powder, cumin and chili powder. Cook uncovered, stirring occasionally, 4 minutes or until vegetables are crisp-tender. Stir in green onions, cilantro, if desired, and brown sugar. *Makes 6 servings*

*Jalapeños can sting and irritate the skin; wear rubber gloves when handling peppers and do not touch eyes. Wash hands after handling.

**Nutrients per Serving:**

| Calories | 67 (30% calories from fat) | | | | |
|---|---|---|---|---|---|
| Total Fat | 3 g | Carbohydrate | 11 g | Iron | 1 mg |
| Saturated Fat | trace | Dietary Fiber | 2 g | Vitamin A | 292 RE |
| Cholesterol | 0 mg | Protein | 2 g | Vitamin C | 91 mg |
| Sodium | 110 mg | Calcium | 40 mg | Sugar | trace |

DIETARY EXCHANGES: 2 Vegetable, ½ Fat

# FESTIVE CORNMEAL BISCUITS

*Another Southern favorite, these biscuits eliminate butter and cream and result in a low-fat treat brimming with heavenly goodness.*

1¾ cups all-purpose flour
½ cup yellow cornmeal
1 tablespoon baking powder
1 tablespoon sugar
1 teaspoon salt
¼ teaspoon baking soda

3 tablespoons margarine
¾ cup buttermilk
1 egg white, beaten
Peach or strawberry preserves
  (optional)

**1** Preheat oven to 425°F. Combine flour, cornmeal, baking powder, sugar, salt and baking soda in large bowl; mix well. Cut in margarine with pastry blender or two knives until mixture forms coarse crumbs. Add buttermilk; mix just until dough holds together.

**2** Turn dough out onto lightly floured surface; knead 8 to 10 times. Pat dough to ½-inch thickness; cut with decorative 2-inch cookie or biscuit cutter. Spray baking sheet with nonstick cooking spray and place biscuits on sheet. Brush tops lightly with beaten egg white.

**3** Bake 12 to 13 minutes or until light golden brown. Serve with preserves, if desired.         *Makes 1 dozen biscuits (1 biscuit per serving)*

**Nutrients per Serving:**

| Calories | 122 (25% calories from fat) | | | | |
|---|---|---|---|---|---|
| Total Fat | 3 g | Carbohydrate | 20 g | Iron | 1 mg |
| Saturated Fat | 1 g | Dietary Fiber | 1 g | Vitamin A | 39 RE |
| Cholesterol | 1 mg | Protein | 3 g | Vitamin C | trace |
| Sodium | 341 mg | Calcium | 38 mg | Sugar | 2 g |

DIETARY EXCHANGES: 1½ Starch/Bread, ½ Fat

# CARROT AND PARSNIP PURÉE

*This simple-to-prepare creation takes ordinary veggies
and transforms them into a creamy delight low in fat but high
in satisfaction. The enticing color will add sparkle to any
holiday table.*

| | |
|---|---|
| 1 pound carrots, peeled | 1 cup clear vegetable broth |
| 1 pound parsnips, peeled | 1 tablespoon margarine |
| 1 cup chopped onion | ⅛ teaspoon ground nutmeg |

**1** Cut carrots and parsnips crosswise into ½-inch pieces.

**2** Combine carrots, parsnips, onion and vegetable broth in medium saucepan. Cover; bring to a boil over high heat. Reduce heat; simmer, covered, 20 to 22 minutes or until vegetables are very tender.

**3** Drain vegetables, reserving broth. Combine vegetables, margarine, nutmeg and ¼ cup reserved broth in food processor. Process until smooth. Serve immediately. *Makes 10 servings*

### Nutrients per Serving:

| Calories | 78 (15% calories from fat) | | | | |
|---|---|---|---|---|---|
| Total Fat | 1 g | Carbohydrate | 16 g | Iron | 1 mg |
| Saturated Fat | trace | Dietary Fiber | 3 g | Vitamin A | 1137 RE |
| Cholesterol | 0 mg | Protein | 1 g | Vitamin C | 8 mg |
| Sodium | 56 mg | Calcium | 35 mg | Sugar | trace |

DIETARY EXCHANGES: 3 Vegetable

### Cook's Tip

If you want to prepare this dish ahead of time, transfer
the completed purée to a microwavable casserole
and chill up to 24 hours. To reheat, microwave
covered at HIGH 6 to 7 minutes, stirring after
4 minutes of cooking.

# ROASTED POTATOES AND PEARL ONIONS

3 pounds red potatoes, well-scrubbed, cut into 1½-inch cubes

1 package (10 ounces) pearl onions, peeled

2 tablespoons olive oil

2 teaspoons dried basil leaves or thyme leaves

1 teaspoon paprika

¾ teaspoon dried rosemary

¾ teaspoon salt

¾ teaspoon ground black pepper

**1** Preheat oven to 400°F. Spray large shallow roasting pan (do not use glass or potatoes will not brown) with nonstick cooking spray.

**2** Add potatoes and onions to pan; drizzle with oil. Combine basil, paprika, rosemary, salt and pepper in small bowl; mix well. Sprinkle over potatoes and onions; toss well to coat with oil and seasonings.

**3** Bake 20 minutes; toss well. Continue baking 15 to 20 minutes or until potatoes are browned and tender.                    *Makes 10 servings*

**Nutrients per Serving:**

| | | | | | | |
|---|---|---|---|---|---|---|
| Calories | 236 (11% calories from fat) | | | | | |
| Total Fat | 3 g | Carbohydrate | 49 g | Iron | 3 mg |
| Saturated Fat | trace | Dietary Fiber | trace | Vitamin A | 16 RE |
| Cholesterol | 0 mg | Protein | 4 g | Vitamin C | 24 mg |
| Sodium | 278 mg | Calcium | 27 mg | Sugar | 1 g |

DIETARY EXCHANGES: 3 Starch/Bread, ½ Fat

### Cook's Tip

To peel pearl onions, cut off the stem end from each onion and plunge the onions into boiling water for 2 minutes; rinse onions in cold water. The skins will slip off.

# MOLASSES BROWN BREAD

*Traditionally served with Boston baked beans, this contemporary take on a New England classic removes the high-fat ingredients yet results in a smooth, sweet and buttery bread.*

1 cup all-purpose flour
1 cup graham or rye flour
1 cup whole wheat flour
1 teaspoon baking soda
½ teaspoon salt
1 cup buttermilk

1 cup light molasses
½ cup golden or dark raisins
½ cup chopped walnuts or
  pecans
Reduced-fat or fat-free cream
  cheese (optional)

**1** Preheat oven to 350°F. Combine all-purpose flour, graham flour, whole wheat flour, baking soda and salt in large bowl. Add buttermilk and molasses; mix well. Stir in raisins and nuts.

**2** Spray 9×5-inch loaf pan with nonstick cooking spray. Spoon batter evenly into pan. Bake 50 to 55 minutes or until wooden pick inserted near center comes out clean.

**3** Transfer pan to wire cooling rack; let stand 10 minutes. Turn bread out onto wire rack; cool completely. Cut into slices. Serve at room temperature with cream cheese, if desired.

*Makes about 18 (½-inch) slices (1 slice per serving)*

**Nutrients per Serving:**

| Calories | 175 (13% calories from fat) | | | | |
|---|---|---|---|---|---|
| Total Fat | 3 g | Carbohydrate | 35 g | Iron | 2 mg |
| Saturated Fat | trace | Dietary Fiber | 2 g | Vitamin A | 3 RE |
| Cholesterol | 1 mg | Protein | 4 g | Vitamin C | trace |
| Sodium | 166 mg | Calcium | 62 mg | Sugar | 17 g |

DIETARY EXCHANGES: 2 Starch/Bread, ½ Fat

# DESSERTS

## CARAMELIZED PEACHES & CREAM

*Divine and dazzling are only two ways to describe this down-home Southern delight. It's a satisfying finale to any holiday feast.*

2 pounds (about 8 medium)
   sliced peeled peaches, or
   thawed and well-drained
   unsweetened frozen peaches
2 tablespoons bourbon
¾ cup reduced-fat sour cream

½ teaspoon ground cinnamon
¼ teaspoon ground nutmeg
¾ cup packed light brown sugar
8 slices (1½ ounces each) angel
   food cake, cut into cubes

**1** Toss peaches with bourbon in shallow ovenproof 1½-quart casserole or 11×7-inch glass baking dish. Press down into even layer.

**2** Combine sour cream, cinnamon and nutmeg in small bowl; mix well. Spoon mixture evenly over peaches. (Mixture may be covered and refrigerated up to 2 hours before cooking time.)

**3** Preheat broiler. Sprinkle brown sugar evenly over sour cream mixture to cover. Broil 4 to 5 inches from heat, 3 to 5 minutes or until brown sugar is melted and bubbly. (Watch closely after 3 minutes so that sugar does not burn.)

**4** Spoon immediately over angel food cake. *Makes 10 servings*

### Nutrients per Serving:

| | | | | | | |
|---|---|---|---|---|---|---|
| Calories | 215 (6% calories from fat) | | | | | |
| Total Fat | 1 g | Carbohydrate | 47 g | Iron | 1 mg |
| Saturated Fat | trace | Dietary Fiber | 1 g | Vitamin A | 117 RE |
| Cholesterol | 6 mg | Protein | 3 g | Vitamin C | 6 mg |
| Sodium | 272 mg | Calcium | 91 mg | Sugar | 8 g |

DIETARY EXCHANGES: 2½ Starch/Bread, ½ Fruit

# MAPLE PUMPKIN PIE

*Nothing says "holidays" like pumpkin pie. The addition of maple syrup gives it a snappy New England accent.*

1⅓ cups all-purpose flour
⅓ cup plus 1 tablespoon sugar, divided
¾ teaspoon salt, divided
2 tablespoons vegetable shortening
2 tablespoons margarine
4 to 5 tablespoons ice water
1 can (15 ounces) solid-pack pumpkin

2 egg whites
1 cup evaporated skimmed milk
⅓ cup maple syrup
1 teaspoon ground cinnamon
½ teaspoon ground ginger
Thawed reduced-fat whipped topping (optional)

**1** Combine flour, 1 tablespoon sugar and ¼ teaspoon salt in medium bowl. Cut in shortening and margarine with pastry blender or two knives until mixture forms coarse crumbs. Mix in ice water, 1 tablespoon at a time, until mixture comes together and forms a soft dough. Wrap in plastic wrap. Refrigerate 30 minutes.

**2** Preheat oven to 425°F. Roll out pastry on floured surface to ⅛-inch thickness. Cut into 12-inch circle. Ease pastry into 9-inch pie plate; turn edge under and flute edge.

**3** Combine pumpkin, remaining ⅓ cup sugar, egg whites, milk, syrup, cinnamon, ginger and remaining ½ teaspoon salt in large bowl; mix well. Pour into unbaked pie shell. Bake 15 minutes; *reduce oven temperature to 350°F.* Continue baking 45 to 50 minutes or until center is set. Transfer to wire cooling rack; let stand at least 30 minutes before serving. Serve warm, at room temperature or chilled with whipped topping, if desired.

*Makes 10 servings*

**Nutrients per Serving:**

| Calories | 198 (22% calories from fat) | | | | |
|---|---|---|---|---|---|
| Total Fat | 5 g | Carbohydrate | 34 g | Iron | 2 mg |
| Saturated Fat | 1 g | Dietary Fiber | 2 g | Vitamin A | 996 RE |
| Cholesterol | 1 mg | Protein | 5 g | Vitamin C | 2 mg |
| Sodium | 231 mg | Calcium | 103 mg | Sugar | 14 g |

DIETARY EXCHANGES: 2 Starch/Bread, 1 Fat

# TROPICAL FRUIT CREAM PARFAITS

*Chock-full of vitamins A, C and D, mangoes are an exotic change
of pace from more commonplace fruits. Tortilla sticks
provide a Southwestern twist.*

1 cup 2% low-fat milk
1 package (4-serving size)
     sugar-free vanilla instant
     pudding mix

½ cup mango nectar
Cinnamon-Ginger Tortilla
     Sticks (recipe follows)
1 large orange, peeled, chopped

**1** Pour milk into medium bowl. Add pudding mix; stir with wire whisk 1 minute or until smooth and thickened. Stir in mango nectar; chill.

**2** Prepare Cinnamon-Ginger Tortilla Sticks. Reserve 10 sticks; divide remaining sticks equally in 5 parfait dishes or small glasses. Top each with pudding mixture, orange and two reserved tortilla sticks.

*Makes 5 servings*

## CINNAMON–GINGER TORTILLA STICKS

3 tablespoons brown sugar
2 tablespoons margarine
½ teaspoon ground ginger

½ teaspoon ground cinnamon
4 (6-inch) flour tortillas, cut
     into ½-inch strips

**1** Preheat oven to 375°F. Combine sugar, margarine, ginger and cinnamon in small microwavable bowl. Microwave at HIGH 1 minute or until smooth when stirred.

**2** Twist tortillas into spirals and arrange on baking sheet sprayed with nonstick cooking spray. Brush each with brown sugar mixture. Bake 10 to 12 minutes or until edges are lightly browned; cool.

*Makes 5 servings*

### Nutrients per Serving:

| Calories | 277 (22% calories from fat) | | | | |
|---|---|---|---|---|---|
| Total Fat | 7 g | Carbohydrate | 51 g | Iron | trace |
| Saturated Fat | 4 g | Dietary Fiber | 1 g | Vitamin A | 84 RE |
| Cholesterol | 16 mg | Protein | 4 g | Vitamin C | 16 mg |
| Sodium | 357 mg | Calcium | 85 mg | Sugar | 5 g |

DIETARY EXCHANGES: ½ Milk, 3 Fruit, 1 Fat

# COCOA HAZELNUT MACAROONS

*To satisfy your holiday sweet tooth without cheating on your diet, bake up a batch of these moist and chewy cookies. Hazelnuts add just the right amount of delicate nuttiness to these tantalizing morsels.*

⅓ cup hazelnuts
¾ cup quick oats
⅓ cup packed brown sugar
6 tablespoons unsweetened
  cocoa powder
2 tablespoons all-purpose flour

4 egg whites
1 teaspoon vanilla
½ teaspoon salt
⅓ cup plus 1 tablespoon
  granulated sugar

**1** Preheat oven to 375°F. Place hazelnuts on baking sheet; bake 8 minutes or until lightly browned. Quickly transfer nuts to dry dish towel. Fold towel; rub vigorously to remove as much of the skins as possible. Finely chop hazelnuts using food processor, nut grinder or chef's knife. Combine with oats, brown sugar, cocoa and flour in medium bowl; mix well. Set aside.

**2** *Reduce oven temperature to 325°F.* Combine egg whites, vanilla and salt in clean dry medium mixing bowl. Beat with electric mixer on high until soft peaks form. Gradually add granulated sugar, continuing to beat on high until stiff peaks form. Gently fold in hazelnut mixture with rubber spatula.

**3** Drop level measuring tablespoonfuls of dough onto cookie sheet. Bake 15 to 17 minutes or until tops of cookies no longer appear wet. Transfer to cooling rack. Store in loosely covered container.

*Makes 3 dozen cookies (3 cookies per serving)*

**Nutrients per Serving:**

| Calories | 104 (24% calories from fat) | | | | |
|---|---|---|---|---|---|
| Total Fat | 3 g | Carbohydrate | 18 g | Iron | 1 mg |
| Saturated Fat | trace | Dietary Fiber | 1 g | Vitamin A | trace |
| Cholesterol | 0 mg | Protein | 3 g | Vitamin C | trace |
| Sodium | 112 mg | Calcium | 22 mg | Sugar | 6 g |

DIETARY EXCHANGES: 1 Starch/Bread, ½ Fat

# MAPLE CARAMEL BREAD PUDDING

*Could bread pudding this creamy and melt-in-your-mouth delicious be low in fat and so easy to prepare? Absolutely!*

8 slices cinnamon raisin bread
2 whole eggs
1 egg white
⅓ cup sugar
1½ cups 2% low-fat milk
½ cup maple syrup

½ teaspoon cinnamon
¼ teaspoon ground nutmeg
¼ teaspoon salt
6 tablespoons fat-free caramel
   ice cream topping

**1** Preheat oven to 350°F. Spray 8×8-inch baking dish with nonstick cooking spray. Cut bread into ¾-inch cubes; arrange in prepared dish.

**2** Beat whole eggs, egg white and sugar in medium bowl. Beat in milk, syrup, cinnamon, nutmeg and salt; pour evenly over bread. Toss bread gently to coat.

**3** Bake 45 minutes or until center is set. Transfer dish to wire cooling rack; let stand 20 minutes before serving. Serve warm with caramel topping.

*Makes 8 servings*

**Nutrients per Serving:**

| | | | | | | |
|---|---|---|---|---|---|---|
| Calories | 235 (12% calories from fat) | | | | | |
| Total Fat | 3 g | Carbohydrate | 47 g | Iron | 1 mg |
| Saturated Fat | 1 g | Dietary Fiber | trace | Vitamin A | 52 RE |
| Cholesterol | 57 mg | Protein | 6 g | Vitamin C | trace |
| Sodium | 228 mg | Calcium | 109 mg | Sugar | 31 g |

DIETARY EXCHANGES: 3 Starch/Bread, ½ Fat

# MOCHA CRINKLES

1¾ cups all-purpose flour
¾ cup unsweetened cocoa
    powder
2 teaspoons instant espresso or
    coffee granules
1 teaspoon baking soda
¼ teaspoon salt

⅛ teaspoon ground black pepper
1⅓ cups packed light brown sugar
½ cup vegetable oil
¼ cup low-fat sour cream
1 egg
1 teaspoon vanilla
½ cup powdered sugar

**1** Mix flour, cocoa, espresso, baking soda, salt and pepper in medium bowl; set aside.

**2** Beat brown sugar and oil in another medium bowl with electric mixer at medium speed until well blended. Beat in sour cream, egg and vanilla.

**3** Beat in flour mixture until soft dough forms. Form dough into disc; cover. Refrigerate dough until firm, 3 to 4 hours.

**4** Preheat oven to 350°F. Place powdered sugar in shallow bowl. Cut dough into 1-inch pieces; roll into balls. Coat with powdered sugar. Place on ungreased cookie sheets.

**5** Bake 10 to 12 minutes or until tops of cookies are firm to the touch. *Do not overbake.* Cool cookies completely on wire racks.

*Makes 6 dozen cookies (1 cookie per serving)*

### Nutrients per Serving:

| | | | | | | |
|---|---|---|---|---|---|---|
| Calories | 44 (30% calories from fat) | | | | | |
| Total Fat | 1 g | Carbohydrate | 7 g | Iron | 1 mg |
| Saturated Fat | trace | Dietary Fiber | 0 g | Vitamin A | 4 RE |
| Cholesterol | 3 mg | Protein | 0 g | Vitamin C | 0 mg |
| Sodium | 28 mg | Calcium | 7 mg | Sugar | trace |

DIETARY EXCHANGES: ½ Starch/Bread

# TURTLE CHEESECAKE

6 tablespoons reduced-calorie margarine
1½ cups graham cracker crumbs
2 envelopes unflavored gelatin
2 packages (8 ounces each) fat-free cream cheese
2 cups 1% low-fat cottage cheese
1 cup sugar

1½ teaspoons vanilla
1 container (8 ounces) thawed reduced-fat nondairy whipped topping
¼ cup prepared fat-free caramel topping
¼ cup prepared fat-free hot fudge topping
¼ cup chopped pecans

**1** Preheat oven to 350°F. Spray bottom and side of 9-inch springform pan with nonstick cooking spray. Melt margarine in small saucepan over medium heat. Stir in graham cracker crumbs. Press crumb mixture firmly onto bottom and side of prepared pan. Bake 10 minutes. Cool.

**2** Place ½ cup cold water in small saucepan; sprinkle gelatin over water. Let stand 3 minutes to soften. Heat gelatin mixture over low heat until completely dissolved, stirring constantly.

**3** Combine cream cheese, cottage cheese, sugar and vanilla in food processor or blender; process until smooth. Add gelatin mixture; process until well blended. Fold in whipped topping. Pour into prepared crust. Refrigerate 4 hours or until set.

**4** Loosen cake from side of pan. Remove side of pan from cake. Drizzle caramel and hot fudge toppings over cake. Sprinkle pecans evenly over top of cake before serving.

*Makes 16 servings*

### Nutrients per Serving:

| | | | | | | |
|---|---|---|---|---|---|---|
| Calories | 231 (26% calories from fat) | | | | | |
| Total Fat | 7 g | Carbohydrate | 33 g | Iron | 1 mg |
| Saturated Fat | 3 g | Dietary Fiber | trace | Vitamin A | 151 RE |
| Cholesterol | 1 mg | Protein | 9 g | Vitamin C | 1 mg |
| Sodium | 419 mg | Calcium | 127 mg | Sugar | 18 g |

DIETARY EXCHANGES: 2 Starch/Bread, ½ Lean Meat, 1 Fat

# APPLE-CRANBERRY TART

*Excellent baking apples such as Jonathan, Jonagold or Rome Beauty are at their peak during the winter months.*

Tart Dough (page 92)
⅓ cup dried cranberries
½ cup boiling water
¾ cup sugar
1 teaspoon ground cinnamon

2 tablespoons cornstarch
4 medium baking apples
Vanilla frozen yogurt
(optional)

**1** Prepare Tart Dough.

**2** Preheat oven to 425°F. Combine cranberries and boiling water in small bowl. Let stand 20 minutes or until softened.

**3** Roll out Tart Dough on floured surface to ⅛-inch thickness. Cut into 11-inch circle. If leftover dough remains, use scraps for decorating top of tart. Ease dough into 10-inch tart pan with removable bottom, leaving ¼ inch of dough above rim of pan. Prick bottom and sides of dough with tines of fork; bake 12 minutes or until dough begins to brown. Cool on wire rack. *Reduce oven temperature to 375°F.*

**4** Combine ¾ cup sugar and cinnamon in large bowl; mix well. Reserve 1 teaspoon mixture for sprinkling over top of tart. Add cornstarch to bowl; mix well. Peel, core and thinly slice apples, adding pieces to bowl as they are sliced; toss well. Drain cranberries. Add to apple mixture; toss well.

**5** Arrange apple mixture attractively over dough. Sprinkle reserved 1 teaspoon sugar mixture evenly over top of tart. Place tart on baking sheet; bake 30 to 35 minutes or until apples are tender and crust is golden brown. Cool on wire rack. Remove side of pan; place tart on serving plate. Serve warm or at room temperature with frozen yogurt, if desired.

*Makes 8 servings*

*continued on page 92*

*Apple-Cranberry Tart, continued*

## TART DOUGH

1⅓ cups all-purpose flour

1 tablespoon sugar

¼ teaspoon salt

2 tablespoons vegetable
  shortening

2 tablespoons margarine

4 to 5 tablespoons ice water

 Combine flour, sugar and salt in medium bowl. Cut in shortening and margarine with pastry blender or two knives until mixture forms coarse crumbs. Mix in ice water, 1 tablespoon at a time, until mixture comes together and forms a soft dough. Wrap in plastic wrap. Refrigerate 30 minutes.

**Nutrients per Serving:**

| | | | | | | |
|---|---|---|---|---|---|---|
| Calories | 263 (22% calories from fat) | | | | | |
| Total Fat | 6 g | Carbohydrate | 50 g | Iron | | 1 mg |
| Saturated Fat | 2 g | Dietary Fiber | 2 g | Vitamin A | | 4 RE |
| Cholesterol | 0 mg | Protein | 2 g | Vitamin C | | 5 mg |
| Sodium | 68 mg | Calcium | 13 mg | Sugar | | 29 g |

DIETARY EXCHANGES: 1½ Starch/Bread, 1½ Fruit, 1½ Fat

❖

### Cook's Tip

The dough can be made in a food processor, but a little care must be taken to avoid a tough crust. Combine the dry ingredients using a few on/off pulses. Add small chunks of cold margarine and use a few more on/off pulses until the mixture resembles small marbles. Add the ice water, again using a few on/off pulses, just until the dough starts to gather on the blade. Turn the mixture out onto a piece of plastic wrap and form the dough into a disk. Refrigerate.

❖

# METRIC CONVERSION CHART

## VOLUME MEASUREMENTS (dry)

$^1/_8$ teaspoon = 0.5 mL
$^1/_4$ teaspoon = 1 mL
$^1/_2$ teaspoon = 2 mL
$^3/_4$ teaspoon = 4 mL
1 teaspoon = 5 mL
1 tablespoon = 15 mL
2 tablespoons = 30 mL
$^1/_4$ cup = 60 mL
$^1/_3$ cup = 75 mL
$^1/_2$ cup = 125 mL
$^2/_3$ cup = 150 mL
$^3/_4$ cup = 175 mL
1 cup = 250 mL
2 cups = 1 pint = 500 mL
3 cups = 750 mL
4 cups = 1 quart = 1 L

## VOLUME MEASUREMENTS (fluid)

1 fluid ounce (2 tablespoons) = 30 mL
4 fluid ounces ($^1/_2$ cup) = 125 mL
8 fluid ounces (1 cup) = 250 mL
12 fluid ounces (1$^1/_2$ cups) = 375 mL
16 fluid ounces (2 cups) = 500 mL

## WEIGHTS (mass)

$^1/_2$ ounce = 15 g
1 ounce = 30 g
3 ounces = 90 g
4 ounces = 120 g
8 ounces = 225 g
10 ounces = 285 g
12 ounces = 360 g
16 ounces = 1 pound = 450 g

## DIMENSIONS

$^1/_{16}$ inch = 2 mm
$^1/_8$ inch = 3 mm
$^1/_4$ inch = 6 mm
$^1/_2$ inch = 1.5 cm
$^3/_4$ inch = 2 cm
1 inch = 2.5 cm

## OVEN TEMPERATURES

250°F = 120°C
275°F = 140°C
300°F = 150°C
325°F = 160°C
350°F = 180°C
375°F = 190°C
400°F = 200°C
425°F = 220°C
450°F = 230°C

## BAKING PAN SIZES

| Utensil | Size in Inches/Quarts | Metric Volume | Size in Centimeters |
|---|---|---|---|
| Baking or Cake Pan (square or rectangular) | 8 × 8 × 2 | 2 L | 20 × 20 × 5 |
| | 9 × 9 × 2 | 2.5 L | 23 × 23 × 5 |
| | 12 × 8 × 2 | 3 L | 30 × 20 × 5 |
| | 13 × 9 × 2 | 3.5 L | 33 × 23 × 5 |
| Loaf Pan | 8 × 4 × 3 | 1.5 L | 20 × 10 × 7 |
| | 9 × 5 × 3 | 2 L | 23 × 13 × 7 |
| Round Layer Cake Pan | 8 × 1$^1/_2$ | 1.2 L | 20 × 4 |
| | 9 × 1$^1/_2$ | 1.5 L | 23 × 4 |
| Pie Plate | 8 × 1$^1/_4$ | 750 mL | 20 × 3 |
| | 9 × 1$^1/_4$ | 1 L | 23 × 3 |
| Baking Dish or Casserole | 1 quart | 1 L | — |
| | 1$^1/_2$ quart | 1.5 L | — |
| | 2 quart | 2 L | — |